FURNESS ABBEY
A HISTORY AND ILLUSTRATED GUIDE

By Alice Leach, B.A.

Alice Leach

Carved head of a king
(external hood of the East Window)
Thought to be King Stephen, the founder of Furness Abbey

Copyright Furness Heritage Press 1988.
Printed by Fletcher & Robinson,
Queen Street, Ulverston.

ISBN   0 9512123 1 1.

D0272956

FOREWORD.

For too long Furness Abbey has remained part of England's "Hidden Heritage"; every year, crowds of visitors make pilgrimages to Glastonbury, Fountains and Rievaulx Abbeys, yet Furness remains relatively unknown. Such was not the case in medieval times for the Abbey of St. Mary of Furness was one of Britain's great religious houses, visited by rich and poor, lords and landowners, prelates and pilgrims – indeed, Furness Abbey became the second richest Cistercian abbey in the kingdom.

In the nineteenth century several guidebooks to the abbey were published and the Furness Railway Company's excursion trains brought tourists to Furness Abbey Station in their thousands; today the influx of visitors is more modest, but surprisingly few modern guidebooks have been produced.

Alice Leach's **Furness Abbey : A History and Illustrated Guide** *has at last redressed this imbalance. Here is an excellent layman's guide which will enlighten and inform. Written in a lively and uncomplicated way, it outlines the history of the abbey and leads the visitor gently round the ruins.*

This book is a labour of love and devotion; it deserves to be widely read just as Furness Abbey deserves to be better known.

William Rollinson,
Senior Lecturer in Geography,
Department of Continuing Education,
University of Liverpool.

In memory of Peggy

ACKNOWLEDGEMENTS.

I would like to acknowledge the help and guidance of Dr. W. Rollinson, M.A. and to thank him for writing the Foreword and allowing me to use some of his maps:

(p. 24) Early Medieval Settlement in Low Furness
Barrow Naturalists' Field Club Proceedings, Vol. IX New Series, 1963, "The Historical Geography of Settlement in Monastic Low Furness," by William Rollinson, M.A.

(p. 25) 'Lands owned by Furness Abbey in the Thirteenth Century'.
("A History of Man in the Lake District") - William Rollinson, M.A.

(p. 35) (i) Bruce's raid on Furness, 1322
Barrow Naturalists' Field Club Proceedings, Vol. IX New Series, 1963, "The Historical Geography of Settlement in Monastic Low Furness," by William Rollinson, M.A.

PHOTOGRAPHY by Roy P. Chatfield, (Pro-Photographics), June 1988, unless otherwise stated.

Arch leading into the Chapter House reproduced on Front Cover and Page 5 by kind permission of the Tourism and Leisure Department, Barrow-in-Furness.

Original photographs of Savigny by Harold Whittaker, 1987.

ART WORK.

Trevor Skempton:
Saint Benedict (iv)
Furness Abbey (p. 4)
Master Mason (p. 10)
Chapter House (p. 45)
Citeaux (p. 47)

Margaret Foran:
Monks in church (p. 16)
Monks seated in Chapter House (p. 23)
Monk leading pack horse (p. 36)
Seal of Furness Abbey (p. 49)

Jo Rose:
Weapons of War (p. 34)

Note on Architecture and Archaeology

The facts in this book relating to the fabric of the building, are based on available evidence at the time of writing.

A large scale survey of all surviving remains is being undertaken (1988), by the Cumbria and Lancashire Archaeological Unit, University of Lancaster, on behalf of English Heritage. Traditionally held views are currently under review.

St. Benedict: the founder of Western Monasticism

Benedict, an Italian nobleman, (born about 480) studied in Rome, before retiring to a mountain at Subiaco, where he lived as a hermit for three years, in the Speco grotto, (see above). Other men joined him, and the band of hermits/monks increased in numbers and twelve monasteries were founded.

About the year 529, Benedict and some of his followers moved to Monte Cassino and built a monastery at the summit of the mountain, on the site of a pagan temple. It was there that Benedict wrote his famous Rule, "the lofty document of Roman wisdom and evangelical spirituality, which was to instruct men and nations in Christian saintliness, 'brotherly love', the habit of work and in the joys of peace and progress"

(The Abbey of Monte Cassino : An Illustrated Guide)

. . . . . . And so the Benedictine Order was born.

Through the ages, members of other religious Orders (both men and women), have adapted the Rule for their particular form of religious life.

The CISTERCIAN ORDER, a reformed Benedictine Order, was founded by Robert of Molesme at Citeaux (1098). St. Bernard, a Cistercian monk, founded the Cistercian Abbey of Clairvaux in 1115, and because of his enormous influence, recruits of all ages and classes joined the Cistercian Order, which was for 200 years one of the most powerful movements in Europe.

INTRODUCTION

For many years after the Norman Conquest, (1066), William I gave land taken from the English, to his Norman barons and knights. They in turn, being deeply religious, gave land, (not the best!) to the Church. Stephen, Count of Boulogne and Mortain, (King of England 1135 - 1154) was one of the many knights to benefit. Following the Norman custom, he made grants of **his** land to the Church — to monks of the Order of Savigny. Thus, these Savigniac monks came into possession of a site at Tulketh, (1124), and the Forest of Furness and Walney, (1127). Stephen then persuaded the Abbot of Savigny to allow a colony of monks to leave their abbey in Savigny, and travel to England, so that he could found the first Savigniac monastery in this country.

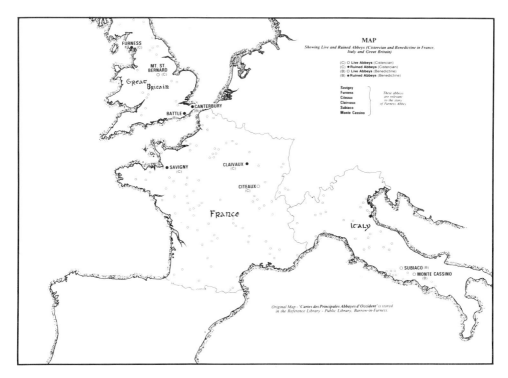

MAP
Showing Live and Ruined Abbeys (Cistercian and Benedictine in France, Italy and Great Britain)

(C) ○ **Live Abbeys** (Cistercian)
(C) ● **Ruined Abbeys** (Cistercian)
(B) ○ **Live Abbeys** (Benedictine)
(B) ● **Ruined Abbeys** (Benedictine)

Savigny
Furness   These abbeys
Citeaux   are relevant
Clairvaux   to the story
Subiaco   of Furness Abbey
Monte Cassino

Original Map - 'Cartes des Principales Abbayes d'Occident' is stored in the Reference Library - Public Library, Barrow-in-Furness.

In 1124, S. Geoffrey, the Abbot of Savigny sent twelve monks from Savigny in France, under the guidance of Ewan d'Avranches, to England. These Savigniac monks, who followed the Rule of St. Benedict, stayed at Tulketh, near Preston, for three years, before moving northwards to the Furness area, where they settled in the Vale of Beckansgill.

1

The Valley of Beckansgill (1) stretches at first to the North and South. It then opens out in a semi-circular sweep before curving round to the east and following the course of the stream.

This valley was lined with New Red Sandstone, from which the abbey was built.

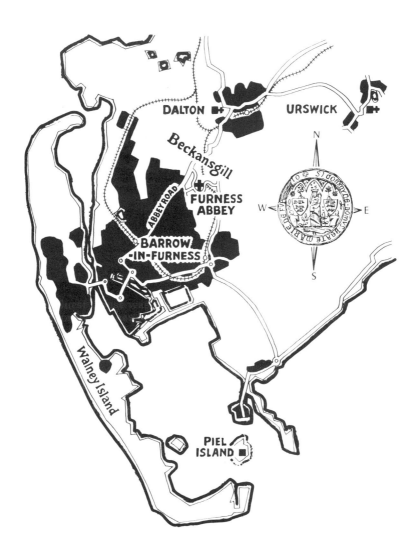

(1) Beckansgill or Beccan's Gill. Beccan is an old Norse name. People of Norse extraction lived in this valley about two hundred years before the arrival of the monks.

Author's comments on colour and form in the Golden Age of the medieval church.

On a recent visit to Gotland, Sweden, I was very impressed by the interiors of the many well preserved medieval churches. Unlike the rest of Europe, the Scandinavian churches did not suffer complete desecration at the Lutheran Reformation. Walls were not whitewashed and many fine statues and precious crucifixes were left untouched, as were magnificent altar pieces and ornate, beautifully carved pulpits and baptismal fonts. All these treasures remain to delight and fascinate the visitor. Many of the wall paintings, illustrating scenes from the Bible and the Lives of Saints, have retained their unique quality of primitive beauty. Columns, arches, pillars, and ceilings are still brilliantly coloured. One is left to gaze in wonder, and to marvel at the talent of the medieval craftsman.

I hope these brief observations will help the reader to develop a mental picture of the Church of St. Mary's of Furness, as it must have looked . . . . in its Golden Age.

A.L.

Wall painting, (medieval church, Gotland)

Furness Abbey, June, 1988.

Arch leading into the Chapter House

A Guided Tour (Using Plan - Outside back cover)

Enter the Abbey grounds through the Museum to begin your tour.

First view of the ruined Abbey of St. Mary's of Furness
In the foreground are the remains of a Guest House and its associated buildings.

The Guest House was laid out here in the twelfth century. The base of a doorway can be seen, on which has been scratched a board for the game of Nine Men's Morris.

S = Remains of a long narrow building thought to have been a stable.

N = Site of board for Nine Men's Morris.

C = Cemetery Gate.

The Cemetery (C) is situated to the east of the church (Ch). Some tombstones remain in their original positions.

Extract from the Foundation Charter.

"In the name of the Blessed Trinity, and in honour of St. Mary of Furness, I Stephen, Earl of Boulogne and Moreton, consulting God, and providing for the safety of my own soul, the soul of my wife, the Countess Matilda, the soul of my lord and uncle, Henry, King of England and Duke of Normandy, and for the souls of all the faithful, living as well as dead, in the year of our Lord 1127, of the Roman Indication, the 5th and 18th of the epact. Considering every day the uncertainty of life, that roses and flowers of kings, emperors and dukes, and the crowns and palms of all the great wither and decay: and that all things, with an uninterrupted course, tend to dissolution and death: I therefore return, give, and grant to God and St. Mary of Furness, all Furness and Walney .... That in Furness an order of regular monks be by Divine permission established: which gift and offering, I, by supreme authority, appoint to be for ever observed; and, that it may remain firm and inviolate for ever, I subscribe this charter with my hand, and confirm it with the sign of the Holy Cross"

The Church (North Transept)
The Porch is approached by the original Main Entrance.

The shield of Furness Abbey with the Abbatial crozier in the centre.

Photo: P. Leach

North Transept   Side Arms   South Transept

MASTER MASON

The monks were not knowledgeable enough to do the designing and building themselves. The workforce would have included carpenters, metalworkers, plumbers, glaziers, tilers and most importantly . . . . . . MASONS.

The master mason was the architect. The FREE masons were the skilled workers. There were also rough masons and labourers.

The church, facing the Transepts and Presbytery.

Look at the plan to find the Quire, Nave, Screen and Altar platform (Chapel). This altar was used by the lay brothers.

The most important building in the monastery was the church, and like all Christian churches, it was built in the shape of a cross.

Photo: A. Leach

Cistercian Monks from Mt. St. Bernard's, Leicestershire,
Furness Abbey, August 14th, 1984
(Left to right : Father Hilary and Brother Peter)

In 1147, at the command of Pope Eugenius III, Serlo, the 4th Abbot of Savigny, surrendered the abbey to St. Bernard, and the Order of Savigny was merged with the great Cistercian Order, (in spite of many disagreements and much bitterness, especially at Furness). Note : Both Savigniacs **and** Cistercians belonged to REFORMED BENEDICTINE Orders.

The first Cistercian Church would have been whitewashed inside and been very stark and simple. Painted wooden crosses were used. The windows were of plain glass.

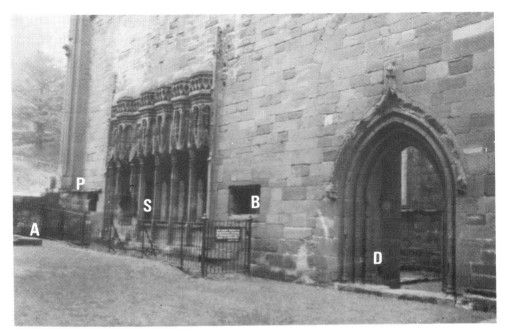

Photo: P. Leach

The main or high altar (A) stood at the eastern end of the presbytery under the East Window. This was where Mass was offered. The four elaborately carved sedilia, (S) one of the abbey's remaining treasures, were reserved for the most reverent monks, such as the abbot, prior, sub-prior or cellarer. Notice the canopied heads and the Tudor flower cresting. The piscina (P) originally had a large stone basin with towel recesses on either side. During the service of the Mass, the priest would have washed his fingers, at the right hand side of the altar, using the inspired words of David, "I will wash my hands among the innocent, and will walk round thy altar O God".

B = aumbry (cupboard)

D = fifteenth century doorway leading to the sacristy where the priest's vestments and sacramental vessels were kept.

Enter the Sacristy and discover the magnificent piscina (small basin with a drain). The altar vessels were washed here.

Belfry Tower

W.W. = West Wall

E. = Entrance to Church

The mighty bell in the Belfry Tower (B.T.) tolled as seven times a day, the monks came to worship and praise their God. They recited the Divine Office which is a public prayer consisting of psalms, hymns and readings from the Bible.

A very special kind of church music was developed for the liturgy, which became prevalent throughout Europe in the eight and ninth centuries. It was called Gregorian Plain Chant, fittingly named after Saint Gregory, who had founded the Roman Cantorum, where the music originated.

The night stairs (S) linked the church with the quire monks' dormitory. These stairs were used by the monks when they came down from their dormitory for the first service of the day.

There is a door from the lay brothers' dormitory from which **their** night stairs led down into the church. This can be seen in the south (twelfth century) wall. (See plan and opposite for West Wall).

Night was not yet over when the prayers of Vigils began. Again at morning and evening they came to church for Lauds and Vespers - the prayers of sunrise and sunset.

Terce was sung at nine o'clock and this was followed by High Mass. This service was conducted either at the high altar under the great East Window, or in one of the side chapels.

A MONK

A monk took vows of Chastity, Poverty and Obedience.

His life's work was God's work - his OPUS DEI, as it was called by St. Benedict. There were two kinds of monks.

(a) The Monachi (the quire monks). The quire monks spent most of their time in the church and the cloister. They were the priests, teachers and scribes of the day. In quire they wore a white woollen cowl, (a large gown with sleeves and hood). The wool from which the garment was woven, was obtained from their own 'Herdwyck' sheep and was not dyed. The Cistercians were therefore known as the WHITE MONKS.

(b) The conversi (the lay brothers). The conversi spent a greater amount of time on manual labour; working in the mills, tanneries, brewhouses and in the fields. They prayed in the church for a few hours each day, or in the places where they worked. Their lives were devoted to prayer and labour (ora et labore). They were the bakers, brewers, maltsters, millers, fullers, blacksmiths, saddlers, foresters, farmers and shepherds of their day.

(This drawing of a monk is taken from Henry Shaw's Sketch Book)

The daily timetable of medieval Cistercian monks.

Rise Vigils	2a.m.
Lauds	Dawn Service
Prime	6a.m.
	(followed by Chapter)
Terce	9.a.m.
	(followed by High Mass)

The hours between services were spent working.

Nones	12 o'clock
	(followed by dinner)
Vespers	4.30p.m.
	(followed by Supper)
Compline	Dusk
	Retire

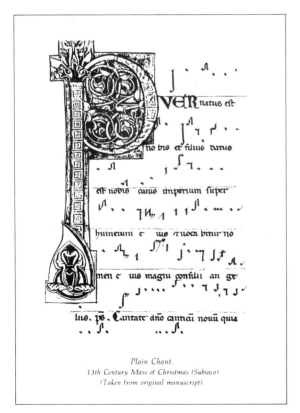

PLAIN CHANT

13th Century Mass of Christmas (Subiaco)

Taken from an original Manuscript.

Plain Chant.
13th Century Mass of Christmas (Subiaco)
(Taken from original manuscript).

"For nearly four hundred years those hallowed walls and Gothic arches echoed with the haunting Plain Chant of the WHITE MONKS of Furness; while a hundred candles lit the Abbey Church".

(Son et Lumiere, '88, Furness Abbey) - A. Leach

The North Transept had an eastern aisle of three bays, (see page 20). In each of the three bays of the aisle was a small chapel and altar. This transept arcade is of typical Cistercian simplicity. Above it is the only open triforium (T) remaining in the abbey. The clerestory (C) or upper storey was a row of windows above the aisle roof which gave light to the central area.

Corbels from above the East Window.

(See pages 40, 41)

The chapel nearest the presbytery has retained its original tiled floor.

P = piscina

T = base of a tomb

Three bays

Enter the Cloister

The Cloister was the abbey's living space. Here the monks walked, meditated and worked. Scribes copied the abbey's charters, perhaps near the North Wall (N.W.) where a place had been set aside for study. Here too, the sons of the abbot's tenants were taught in the Abbey School.

The monastery had to provide for all the needs of the community of brothers. The main buildings were built around the Cloister Court (A); the kitchen, refectory, dormitory, parlour and warming room.

B = a covered alley which went round all four sides of the cloister

LD = lay brothers' dormitories.

R = lay brothers' refectory. Their latrines (reredorters) were situated on the western side of the cloister.

On Sundays and Feast Days, a procession left the church by door (N), walked round the cloister and re-entered by door (D).

The holes in the wall were made for the timber used in building the 'lean to' roof of the covered alley. The floor would have been made of sandstone.

The Five Glorious Arches

2 Arches (Bc) were the book cupboards

Arch (Ch) led into the Chapter House
Arch (P) was the parlour where the monks could talk, and break their vow of silence for a
    short time.

Arch (E) was the slype (a passage)

D = Quire brothers' dormitories

The Warming House (see Plan), was a square room with a fireplace. The brothers were
allowed to spend specific times there in very cold weather.

The Chapter House

Notice the twin lancet windows (L.W.) and the elaborate medallions (M) between their heads.

Each morning, after Mass, the abbot and his monks filed into the Chapter House, so called, because a Chapter from St. Benedict's Rule was read aloud. This was followed by prayers for the souls of the dead.

But this room was also a parliament - a court - in fact it was the Power House, where important monastic business was discussed, and Charters were granted.

The abbot sat in his high stone seat, while everyone took his seat in order, from the oldest, down to the newest novice.

23

THE ABBEY'S WEALTH.

From the twelfth to the sixteenth century, there was a great increase in the fortunes of the monks of Furness, (in spite of the fact that vows of poverty had been taken).

The abbey's great riches came from the acquisition of land (by gift and purchase), from sheep and cattle farming, and from the mining of ore.

The monks of Furness were successful farmers.
The lay brothers brought marshland and wasteland into productive use. "Between 1127 and 1220 the Furness Abbey monks brought into cultivation some 2000 acres of arable land" (V.C.H.)

The monks of Furness were astute business men.
In 1209 they bought Borrowdale from Alice de Remelli for £156. 13s. 4d. and 2 "stirks", making another sheep pasture.

The monks of Furness were great landowners.
(1322) "The monks of Saint Mary's have hitherto rapidly accumulated territorial possessions through the pious bequest of individuals of all grades; among their ample stores are garnered equally the donations of the prince and the peasant; their estates in England are now numerous, extended and productive" (T.A. Beck)

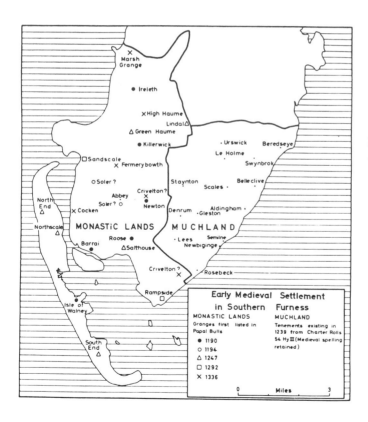

(See page 45 for information relating to Granges)

Reproduced by kind permission of Dr. W. Rollinson, M.A.

24

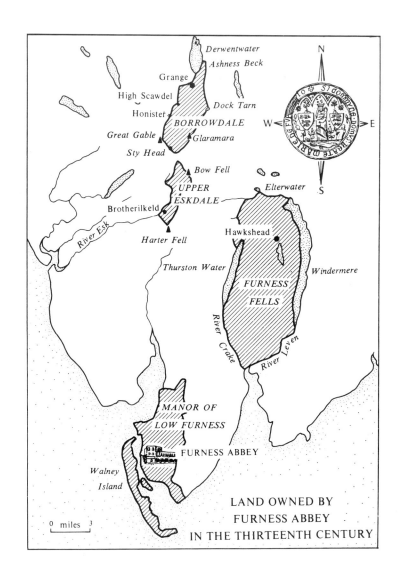

Reproduced by kind permission of Dr. W. Rollinson, M.A.

Between the years 1127 and 1537, the abbey gained a great deal of land in the Lake District. All the land between Coniston Water and Windermere was owned by the monks, who converted the land into a sheep pasture.

Furness Abbey also owned land in Yorkshire.
"The great slopes of Whernside and Ingleborough were dotted with sheep belonging to the Abbey" (V.C.H.)

25

The vaulted UNDERCROFT was used for storing wine, food and other necessary items.
It was built under the dormitory (dorter)

However, as this room is the largest of its kind in England, it could have had a dual purpose.
Perhaps it was also used as a library or a Common Room.

The remains of the quire monks' latrines are to the East.
They were built over the stream and reached by a passage at first floor level.

View of the stream with east end of Infirmary complex.

THE INFIRMARY.

The Infirmary Chapel (C) has retained its original vault (span of 25 ft. - 7.6m.) Notice the unusual triangular headed windows.
Inside the chapel there is a stone wall bench, and a fine piscina.

The large Infirmary Hall (A) - (the Hospital Ward), measured 126ft x 47ft (38 x 14m). The heads of the beds fitted into the recesses round the walls and there was a large double fireplace in the south wall. The infirm were able to reach the Warming House by a connecting passage and doorway.

The Infirmary was a miniature monastery, for it had its own Chapel, kitchen, buttery, and latrines for the patients . . . . . . the sick and . . . . . . the terminally ill. Thus it was at the same time the FIRST HOSPITAL . . . . . . and . . . . . . the FIRST HOSPICE in Furness.

28

The Amphitheatre Field

The outline of a sledgeway (S) can still be seen in the present day amphitheatre. Sledges, drawn by oxen were used to carry the heavy blocks of sandstone from the quarry to the building site in the abbey grounds. Wheeled vehicles of that era would have been very crude and would not have withstood the weight of stones.

Mortar was made by mixing lime, sand and horse hair fibres.

Furness Abbey's Fish Farm

Furness Abbey had extensive fishing rights. The Duddon and other streams provided fish which was dragged from the River Lune and stored in the fish pond at Beaumont Grange. Fish was also brought from the sea and kept in the abbey's fish ponds. The flat floor of the amphitheatre - the present day football pitch, is the site of the abbey's fish 'farm'.

From the early days of the abbey, the abbots had fishing boats on Coniston and Windermere Lakes.

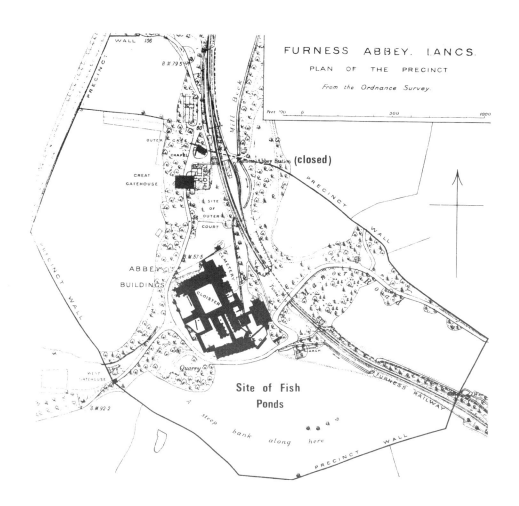

FURNESS ABBEY. LANCS.

PLAN OF THE PRECINCT

From the Ordnance Survey.

(closed)

View of the Infirmary complex from the Abbotswood Nature Trail

Abbot's Seal

Abbot means 'Father', and the title was used from earliest times for the head of a monastery. The word 'abbey' was derived from it.

The octagonal kitchen was next to the Infirmary Chapel
Look out for a water trough, hearths for fire places, and a rubbish chute discharging into the beck.
A doorway and passage connected the Infirmary with the thirteenth century kitchen.

The remains of a trough

'Gargoyle type sculpture'
Gargoyles are water spouts, projecting from the parapet of a wall or tower, often carved into human or animal shapes.

Across the beck, set against the side of the valley, was the ABBOT'S HOUSE (former mid-thirteenth century infirmary)

There are remains of a large central fireplace (F) in the eastern wall. Notice the twin lancet windows (LW)

Robert Bruce slept here? . . . . . . Read on . . . . . .

Scottish soldiers raided the Furness area twice, in 1316, and again, in 1322.

THE GREAT RAID (1322)

Robert Bruce and his men invaded England, through Carlisle. Holme Cultram Abbey was plundered, before the Scots crossed the Duddon Sands and arrived at Furness Abbey. Abbot John Cockerham, the twenty fourth Abbot, heard that Robert Bruce was on his way, and went to meet him. He paid him ransom money on condition that the abbey lands should not again be burnt or plundered. Robert Bruce spent the night at the abbey, probably staying in the Abbot's House, before crossing the sands of Morecambe Bay at low water. The Scots left Cartmel in ruins, burnt Lancaster town (except the castle), and returned by way of Carlisle, reaching Scotland on July 24th, with great booty and many prisoners.

This drawing illustrates the weapons of war used in the Great Raid.

It is a modification, based on the initial letter of Edward II's Charter of Carlisle 12th May, 1316.

"They seized all the manufactured iron that they could find and carried it off with the greatest of joy, although so heavy of carriage and preferred it to other plunder". (The Chronicle of Lanercost").

A legend claims that the Mater Dolorosa (Mother of Sorrows statue), on the Tower of Urswick Church, commemorates the people who were killed in the Great Raid.

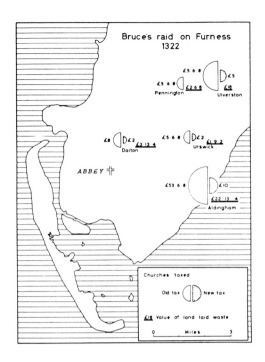

Reproduced by kind permission of Dr. W. Rollinson, M.A.

Before the Great Raid, most of the parishes in the area had paid quite respectable sums of money towards the building of St. Peter's (Peter's Pence). But twenty years after the Great Raid, witness the difference by studying the following table.

Peter's Pence

Before the Great Raid	After the Great Raid
Dalton sent £8.	Dalton sent £2.
Aldingham sent £53-6s.-8d.	Aldingham sent £10.
Pennington sent £5-6s.-9d.	Pennington sent £2-6s.-8d.

The Scots had destroyed peoples' homes and livelihoods. Famine and disease spread through the land, and much hardship was caused.

Piel Castle from the North West.

(Courtesy of Furness Collection)

This "dwelling house" dated back to the early days of the abbey. It was a walled WAREHOUSE, where wool and wine were stored, before being shipped overseas.

Many castles were built as a direct result of the Scottish wars. Piel Castle and Dalton Castle formed part of the defensive system, and were similar to those built in various parts of the Border country, e.g. Sizergh Castle, Great Salkeld Rectory, and Raiseholme Tower, near Arnside. Only a few years after the Great Raid, in 1327, the Abbot of Furness decided to . . . . "crenellate his dwelling house on the Isle of Fotheray", i.e. to build Piel Castle as a fortification against any future Scottish raids. These three storied massively built PELE towers provided a refuge from sudden attacks. The walls varied in thickness (from 3 feet to 10 feet). The roof was normally flat so that arrows could be fired at the raiders.

Lay brother and noviciates were recruited from the local inhabitants. Here is a conjectural view of a lay brother leading a pack horse, which could be carrying wool to Piel Island for storage, before being shipped to France.

Dalton Castle Drawn by C. Cuitt. Engraved by W. Hughes.

(Courtesy of Furness Collection)

Dalton Castle probably replaced an earlier building on this site, which had been used as a prison and court house, controlled by the abbots of Furness. This was their headquarters - their H.Q.

"The little borough of Dalton was six times in the year, the scene of a busy fair, which brought distant merchants, to quicken trade, and gave dues to the Abbey". (V.C.H.)

THE COUCHER BOOKS.

The Coucher Books are primary sources for the History of Furness Abbey. In 1412, Abbot William Dalton decided to keep a permanent record of Furness Abbey's possessions and other important matters.

All the charters relating to the abbey were copied or "couched". The monks wrote on parchment, using quill pens, and black and coloured ink with decorative gold leaf, for their beautiful illustrations and emblazoned heraldic devices. John Stell was one of the scribes, and he included his own portrait as an illuminated letter. (See inside cover).

A monk of Furness seeking the protection of the Virgin Mary, patroness of the Abbey.
From the Furness Coucher Book DL42/3 (Reproduced by kind permission of the Public Record Office, Kew, Richmond, Surrey).

On your tour of Furness Abbey, remember that History is all around you; on the ground, on the ruined walls, and on the tops of pillars and arches. It is important not to forget to look up.

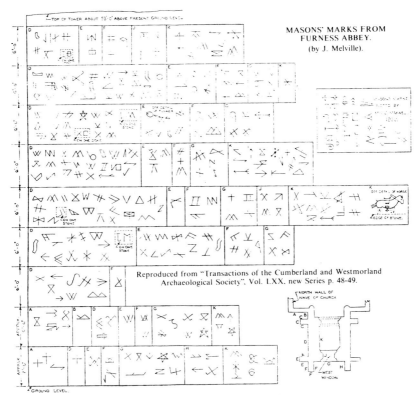

MASONS' MARKS FROM
FURNESS ABBEY.
(by J. Melville).

Reproduced from "Transactions of the Cumberland and Westmorland Archaeological Society", Vol. LXX, new Series p. 48-49.

"HISTORY ON THE WALLS".

The masons of Solomon's Temple were said to have been provided with a peculiar mark which was placed on their work. Thus each mason's work would be easily recognisable and any piece of defective workmanship detected.

The masons of Furness Abbey left their trade marks - their signatures.

The flower which looks rather like a tulip, is interesting, because this flower was not introduced to Western Europe from Turkey, until some time after the Dissolution of the Monasteries.

This is not likely to be post-monastic 'doodling', as it is about 30ft above ground level. It covers the whole face of the stone. (Binoculars are necessary).

Re-enter the church with your binoculars.

"HISTORY ABOVE YOU"

Look to the top of the walls to find these corbels. A corbel is a block of stone, often elaborately carved, projecting from a wall. It supports the beams of a roof, floor, vault, or other feature. Inspiration for this particular type of ecclesiastical sculpture was often drawn from the twelfth and thirteenth century bestiaries. These semi-religious books contained pictures of animals, birds and reptiles, with annotations describing their nature and habits. Each animal represented a particular Christian moral. Thus the camel, which kneels to receive its load, was taken as a type of Christ, while the dormouse symbolised sloth. A wild boar was the symbol for a cruel and worldly prince.

The first craftsmen who carved these creatures did so in a spirit of religious zeal and were fully conscious of the inherent symbolism, but towards the end of the thirteenth century, their work became purely decorative, as Gothic architecture, with its qualities of simplicity and austerity, was replaced by the more sophisticated 'decorated' style.

These lozenge shaped stones came from the Savigniac Church — the first Church at Furness.

Vitalis, known as the hermit saint, was born in Tierceville near Bayeux in 1050. In the year 1112, Henry I, King of England and Normandy, gave Vitalis and his fellow hermits the forest of Savigny and the remains of a castle. In that same year, Vitalis founded the Order of Savigny and the first Savigniac monastery. The men who joined the new Order were called Savigniac monks. They wore grey habits and followed the Rule of St. Benedict. In 1147, all Savigniac monasteries were merged with the great Cistercian Order (See page 12) They were destroyed by the French revolutionaries. The Cistercian Abbey of Savigny was dissolved in 1792.

All that remains of what must once have been a noble abbey. A stone altar has been erected over the site of the last altar, in front of which stands a stone effigy of a monk (Vitalis ?)

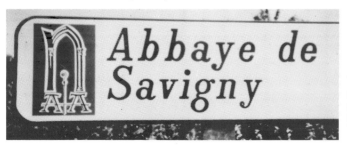

The 18th century high altar in the collegiate church of Saint Evroult (Mortain), came from L'Abbaye de Savigny.

The shrine in honour of Mary is interesting, and serves as a reminder that all Cistercian abbeys were dedicated to the Virgin Mary.

"Mary presided here at the prayer of the monks, sons of Vitalis, for 680 years (1112 - 1792). She has protected our parish during the war (1939-45)"

This evidence proves conclusively that this was indeed the site of the first Savigniac monastery. Ewan d'Avranches and his twelve monks left here in 1124 to establish the first Savigniac monastery in England, first at Tulketh (1124), and then at Furness (1127). (See page 1)

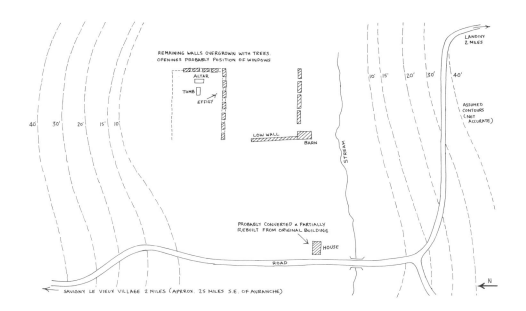

The ruins of L'Abbaye de Savigny are located two miles east of the village of Savigny Le Vieux and 20 miles S.E. of Avranches.

Tomb with effigy (St. Vital - Vitalis?)

Re-enter Chapter House.

The management of Granges was an important issue and would almost certainly be a subject for debate at the 'Chapter'. These granges or home farms were large farm settlements, worked by the lay brothers, under the supervision of the master of the granges (grangiarius), who kept in close contact with the monastery and its cellarer. The granges provided the abbey with grain, pigs and other produce.
Later on these granges grew into villages, or in the case of Barrow, a major town.

*(See map,
page 24)*

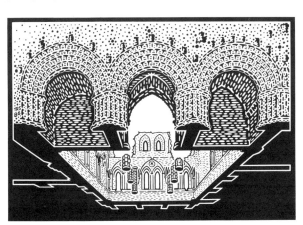

THE GOLDEN AGE (1342 - 1537)

As more and more wealth poured into the abbey's treasury, many Cistercian Rules were ignored. Fine sculptured statues (1) filled every niche and moulded figures decorated pillars and vaulted roofs. Magnificent sedilia had exquisitely carved canopied heads.

Altar frontals were of cloth of gold with gold embroidered icons. There were silver chalices and golden monstrances, while priests were resplendent in bejewelled copes.

One can only imagine the beauty of the windows:
"rich crimsons, vibrant azures, and glowing emerald greens of glorious stained glass illumined St. Mary of Furness".

The noble abbey stood . . . . a monument to the POWER of man . . . . and
the GLORY of God.

(Son et Lumiere - Furness Abbey '88' - A. Leach)

(1) The projecting buttresses of the West Tower have elaborately gabled canopies and bases for statues.

THE DECLINE (1342 - 1537)

But the Golden Age did not last. The Black Death (1347 - 1350) and subsequent plagues, caused widespread upheaval to the Cistercians, especially the lay brothers; a blow from which they were never to recover. Farms were no longer tended, cattle and sheep lay dead in the fields. Fewer and fewer men joined the Order. Vows of poverty were frequently forgotten, and, in general, monasteries no longer resembled St. Benedict's "Households of God".

Furness Abbey must have gained a fairly poor reputation during the abbacy of Alexander Bankes. He destroyed Sellergarth Village and appeared in the Duchy Court at least twelve times between 1509 and 1531, being the defendant in eight cases, usually because he had attempted to gain fisheries by force or dishonesty. The abbey at this period seems to have been functioning more like a property company than a religious community . . . . Then came the death knell . . . . THE DISSOLUTION OF THE MONASTERIES.

Between 1529 and 1536, in the wake of the Lutheran Reformation and his own matrimonial problems, Henry VIII commanded Parliament to pass various acts which completely changed the way in which the English church was governed. As the new Head of the Church in England, following his break with the Church of Rome, the king issued an order for the closing down of the monasteries; his main objective being to acquire their great wealth.

The Church of Citeaux Abbey. (Notice the stark simplicity)

The French Revolutionaries expelled the fifty-two remaining monks in 1791 from Citeaux (the Mother House). The abbey's treasures were sold, the twelfth century church and the cloister dismantled, the books and manuscripts, dispersed. After a chequered history, the church was re-built in 1846 and to-day the splendid Abbey of Citeaux, (risen like a phoenix from the ashes), is still the mother house of the Cistercians.

Corbel (a monk's face), to be seen on the Sacristy wall.

Henry VIII's adviser, Thomas Cromwell, appointed a Commission of Ecclesiastical lawyers to visit all monasteries. Their official reports reveal that monastic vows were kept and religious practices observed in many great monasteries, but that some small monasteries were corrupt.

Abbot Roger Pele and three monks of Furness were charged with immorality. However, Furness Abbey had no relics to attract pilgrims like Conishead Priory and Calder Abbey, and there is no evidence that St. Mary's of Furness was hopelessly corrupt.

The Commissioners had made whirlwind visits over just a few months, visiting over five hundred abbeys. They merely scheduled charges without investigation. The reader can draw his own conclusions!!!

The DEED OF SURRENDER was signed at Furness Abbey, in the Chapter House, by Abbot Roger Pele and 29 monks on April 9th 1537.

"In witness whereof we have with our unanimous and full assent and consent affixed our common seal to these presents. Given in the Chapter House of our said monastery, the ninth day of April, in the twenty-eighth year of the reign of our said lord and king, and in the year of our Lord and Saviour, one thousand five hundred and thirty seven". (Extract from the Surrender Document).

'The Common Seal of St. Mary's of Furness'

Following the king's instructions, the demolition 'work' began. Thomas Holcroft was in charge of making Furness Abbey uninhabitable, beginning with the church. He employed labourers, and paid them £70 in wages to pull down the buildings and provided them with ropes and "engines". These medieval engines consisted of a whole collection of wooden siege implements. A type of scaffolding would have been used so that the lead could be removed from the roof. Precious altar vessels, priest's richly embroidered vestments and other treasures became the property of the Crown. As windows were smashed, the beautiful stained glass broke into thousands of fragments, of which only a few have survived e.g. Urswick Church, (see the lancet window) and St. Mary's Parish Church Dalton, where some pieces have been set into the modern windows.

A carved head
of a queen —
Mathilda?

The following entry was made in the King's Receiver's account for 1536-8, "also paid for the carriage of three 'packs' of evidence and books of the lands and possessions of the late monastery from Furness to London, upon three horses, together with hemp and other packing needed for the safe carriage". These records of the abbey's history were later bound together into two volumes and called the Coucher Books (see page 38).

The abbot was made Vicar of Dalton Church. Three sick and old monks who had lived in the infirmary were turned out with £3 each. The quire monks who could not obtain clerical jobs, became tutors, while the lay brothers went back to working on the land. The boys in the Cloister School were sent home. Workmen, both skilled and unskilled, were paid their wages and dismissed. Most of the poor people (including 8 widows), who had been fed daily, received nothing, while 13 poor patients from the hospital, were given 13 shillings and 4 pence, and sent away to depend on charity.

This was the end of an era. Life would never be the same again.

The monks' cemetery lay east of the church. King Reginald II of Man is buried here. Rushen Abbey on the Isle of Man was a daughter abbey of Furness Abbey, as were Calder, Swineshead, Iniscourcey, and Wyresdale.

Medieval cross inscribed on one of the graves.

Look up to find the carved heads of a king and queen (thought to be Stephen and Mathilda), moulded to the external hood of the Great East Window (see page (i) and page 50).

The North Transept, from the east, showing the triple arcade.

Exit through the Museum to the car park, where there are some remains of the great 12th cer. ury gatehouse.   Turn right.

There was a chapel, outside the gatehouse for lay people.

A = Altar

S = Sedilia

B = base of a large statue.

The building (first mentioned in 1344), was called the Capella Extra Portas,
(Chapel outside the gate)

Pilgrims visited this Chapel, where there was a statue of the Virgin Mary. Before that date, the statue was venerated in the North Transept.

After your tour of the Abbey ruins, you may like to make a small detour to Ennis Wood to see Bow Bridge.

This medieval bridge is south of the Infirmary, about 600 yards downstream. It was built across the stream when New Mill was built in Bekan's Gill. The monks established at least four waterpowered Corn mills; Orgrave (between Marton and Dalton), Little Mill, below Mill Brow (called Breastmill), and New Mill, just outside the precinct wall, below the infirmary.

The Abbey has been owned by several families since its dissolution – namely, the Prestons, the Lowthers and finally the Cavendishes.   In 1923, Lord Richard Cavendish placed the ruins in the guardianship of the Office of Works (now under the care of English Heritage), for preservation as a national monument.

You may leave the abbey precinct by the Western Gate.

Thankyou for your visit to the ruined Abbey of St. Mary's of Furness, where you have been a most welcome guest. Perhaps one day, you will return to the lovely Vale of Beckansgill.